Written by
Cyndie Jacks and Dawn Lewis

Contributions by Patrice Brake, Amy Bronson,
Andrea Douglass, Jeni McCarrell,
Sherry Sickler, and Kayla Venner

Editor: Sheri Rous
Illustrator: John Jones
Cover Illustrator: Greg Moraes
Designer: Terri Lamadrid
Cover Designer: Terri Lamadrid
Art Director: Tom Cochrane
Project Director: Carolea Williams

Table of Contents

Introduction

Is test-prep practice squeezing the life out of your classroom? Have you let valuable activities such as reading a good book slip by to make room for more worksheets and drill? Now you can bring these valuable activities back into the classroom and still have time for test-prep practice. *Test Prep with a Twist* combines children's literature with activities that introduce and review key concepts that students need to know to perform well on standardized tests. After students review these key concepts, use the practice tests to help you assess student needs and help familiarize students with the multiple-choice test-taking format.

This easy-to-use resource contains 20 mini-units. Each mini-unit features a literature synopsis, an activity, and a student practice test.

Literature
By using favorite literature selections as "hooks" to generate interest, students will learn and review skills without feeling overwhelmed by the pressure that test preparation often brings. When you use literature to introduce or review a concept, students see the application of the concept rather than just studying it in isolation.

Group Activities
The activities tie in the literature selections with a specific language arts concept. Students will engage in high-interest learning while you teach and reinforce basic skills.

Practice Tests
The practice tests help prepare students for the format they will encounter on standardized tests. By introducing students to test formats and skills, they will gain confidence with test-taking procedures.

Additional Features
In addition to the mini-units, there are three cumulative tests to assess student knowledge of each concept, test-taking tips, record and answer sheets, and an answer key.

Implement the activities in *Test Prep with a Twist* and watch your classroom spring back to life!

Getting Started

Test-Taking Resources

This book is divided into three main sections: Comprehension, Grammar, and Vocabulary. Each section provides literature selections, activities, and test-taking practice pages that are designed similar to standardized tests. Follow these simple steps to maximize your students' test-taking practice:

✓ Familiarize yourself with the Table of Contents, which includes the concepts and literature titles presented in this resource.

✓ Copy onto a large piece of chart paper the Test-Taking Tips reproducible (page 5), and display it in the classroom. Review on numerous occasions the tips presented on the chart to maximize student test-taking preparation. Copy the Test-Taking Bookmarks (page 6) onto card stock, and cut them out. Give each student a bookmark, and encourage students to review the tips listed on it during free time.

✓ Make a copy of the Teacher Record Sheet (page 7). For easy reference, list each student's name at the top of the sheet, and record in the appropriate box the score for each student's practice test and culminating test. Use this sheet as a tool for tracking student progress.

✓ Select a concept that you want students to practice. Read the corresponding teacher page, which contains the synopsis and activity directions. Gather the appropriate children's book to read to the class, and follow the activity directions. Then, have students complete the accompanying activity.

✓ Copy the corresponding practice test for the unit on which students are currently working. As an option, copy the Student Answer Sheet (page 8) for students to practice transferring answers onto an answer sheet. The answer sheet also works well with any teacher-made tests. Allow students 5–10 minutes, depending on student ability level, to complete the practice test. Review answers with the entire class. The practice test can be administered the same day as the activity or at a later date as time permits.

✓ After you have taught or reviewed all the concepts and have administered the practice tests, give each student the final review tests on pages 57–62. Allow students 20–30 minutes to complete each test. The final review tests can be given to students all at the same time or on separate days.

Test-Taking Tips

✓ Listen carefully when the teacher explains the directions.

✓ Read any titles or picture captions first.

✓ Watch for a change in directions. They may change within the same section of the test.

✓ Answer the questions you know first. Leave the hard ones for later.

✓ Read all the choices—even after you think you have found the right choice.

✓ Read each choice as if it were a true or false statement. Select the choice that is true.

✓ Use common sense. Ignore the obviously wrong choices. Look at the good choices carefully to pick the one that best answers the question.

✓ Use context clues. Study all the pictures and graphics before answering the question.

✓ Take your time. Carefully think about similar choices.

✓ Be careful of statements that use words such as *always, never,* and *sometimes.*

✓ Decide what the question really asks. Ignore unimportant information.

✓ If time permits, recheck your answers. Do not change an answer without good reason.

✓ Relax!

Test-Taking Bookmarks

Test-Taking Tips
- ✓ Answer the questions you know first. Leave the hard ones for later.
- ✓ Read all the choices—even after you think you have found the right choice.
- ✓ Use common sense. Ignore the obviously wrong choices. Look at the good choices carefully to pick the one that best answers the question.
- ✓ If time permits, recheck your answers. Do not change an answer without good reason.
- ✓ Relax!

Test-Taking Tips
- ✓ Answer the questions you know first. Leave the hard ones for later.
- ✓ Read all the choices—even after you think you have found the right choice.
- ✓ Use common sense. Ignore the obviously wrong choices. Look at the good choices carefully to pick the one that best answers the question.
- ✓ If time permits, recheck your answers. Do not change an answer without good reason.
- ✓ Relax!

Test-Taking Tips
- ✓ Answer the questions you know first. Leave the hard ones for later.
- ✓ Read all the choices—even after you think you have found the right choice.
- ✓ Use common sense. Ignore the obviously wrong choices. Look at the good choices carefully to pick the one that best answers the question.
- ✓ If time permits, recheck your answers. Do not change an answer without good reason.
- ✓ Relax!

Test-Taking Tips
- ✓ Answer the questions you know first. Leave the hard ones for later.
- ✓ Read all the choices—even after you think you have found the right choice.
- ✓ Use common sense. Ignore the obviously wrong choices. Look at the good choices carefully to pick the one that best answers the question.
- ✓ If time permits, recheck your answers. Do not change an answer without good reason.
- ✓ Relax!

Test Prep with a Twist • Gr. 3 © 2003 Creative Teaching Press

Teacher Record Sheet

Student Name																		Page	Practice Tests
																		10	Cause and Effect
																		12	Making Inferences
																		14	Making Inferences
																		17	Sequencing
																		19	Sequencing
																		21	Setting
																		24	Story Elements
																		27	Adjectives
																		29	Adjectives: Superlatives
																		31	Capitalization
																		33	Contractions
																		36	Periods and Question Marks
																		38	Verbs
																		41	Verb Tenses
																		43	Antonyms
																		45	Context Clues
																		48	Homonyms
																		50	Multiple Meanings of Words
																		53	Synonyms
																		56	Vocabulary Development
																			Final Review Tests
																		57	The Zoo
																		59	Alli and Abby
																		61	Apple Crisp

Getting Started

Test Prep with a Twist • Gr. 3 © 2003 Creative Teaching Press

Student Answer Sheet

Name	Name
_____	_____
Date	Date
_____	_____

1. (a) (b) (c) (d)   1. (a) (b) (c) (d)

2. (a) (b) (c) (d)   2. (a) (b) (c) (d)

3. (a) (b) (c) (d)   3. (a) (b) (c) (d)

4. (a) (b) (c) (d)   4. (a) (b) (c) (d)

5. (a) (b) (c) (d)   5. (a) (b) (c) (d)

6. (a) (b) (c) (d)   6. (a) (b) (c) (d)

7. (a) (b) (c) (d)   7. (a) (b) (c) (d)

8. (a) (b) (c) (d)   8. (a) (b) (c) (d)

9. (a) (b) (c) (d)   9. (a) (b) (c) (d)

10. (a) (b) (c) (d)   10. (a) (b) (c) (d)

11. (a) (b) (c) (d)   11. (a) (b) (c) (d)

12. (a) (b) (c) (d)   12. (a) (b) (c) (d)

Test Prep with a Twist • Gr. 3 © 2003 Creative Teaching Press

That's Good! That's Bad!

Written by Margery Cuyler
(Henry Holt and Company)

Synopsis

Through a series of adventures and misadventures, a little boy's stroll through the city zoo turns into a walk on the wild side! This story shows how a number of cause and effect scenarios create both good and bad situations for the boy.

Activity

Prepare an accordion book for each pair of students by folding a 12" x 36" (30.5 cm x 1 m) piece of construction paper lengthwise. Then, fold it into equal segments "accordion-style." Read *That's Good! That's Bad!* to the class, and draw students' attention to the seemingly good or bad events that hinge upon one another. Discuss with the class how the reader anticipates the good things and dreads the bad things that the little boy experiences in the story. Explain that each action in the story creates a reaction called "cause and effect." Challenge students to share as many cause and effect scenarios from the story that they can find. Record student responses on the board. Divide the class into pairs. Give each pair an accordion book. Have students use the pattern of text from the story to create an imaginative cause and effect mini-story of their own. Invite them to write and illustrate their story on each page of their book. Invite partners to share their story with the class.

Materials
- *That's Good! That's Bad*
- construction paper
- crayons or markers

Test Practice

Give each student a Cause and Effect practice test (page 10). Give students 5–10 minutes to complete the test. Review the answers with the entire class.

Cause and Effect

Directions: Read each **cause** sentence. Choose the answer that tells the **effect** of the **cause**.

1. I set out a mousetrap with cheese.
   - (a) I scraped my knee.
   - (b) We ate dinner.
   - (c) A mouse was caught.
   - (d) It was raining.

2. We drove our car through the mud.
   - (a) I saw a butterfly.
   - (b) We needed a car wash.
   - (c) The cows were eating.
   - (d) It snowed last night.

3. Kim forgot to water the plant.
   - (a) The plant died.
   - (b) The sun came out.
   - (c) The girl rode her bike.
   - (d) The cat napped.

4. I tripped on a rock.
   - (a) It was a windy day.
   - (b) The boys swam fast.
   - (c) My stomach hurt.
   - (d) I scraped my knee.

5. Mom poured the cake batter into the pan.
   - (a) She poured the milk.
   - (b) Mom worked in the yard.
   - (c) She went upstairs.
   - (d) Mom baked the cake.

6. I ate too much ice cream and cake at the party.
   - (a) I had a stomachache.
   - (b) The children were noisy.
   - (c) The teacher was nice.
   - (d) We played tag.

7. The ham was left out of the refrigerator overnight.
   - (a) We picked strawberries.
   - (b) The children were hungry.
   - (c) The ham spoiled.
   - (d) It was raining.

8. We drove to the beach.
   - (a) The horse was grazing.
   - (b) We went swimming in the ocean.
   - (c) Dad used the computer.
   - (d) I made the bed.

Everyday Mysteries

Written by Jerome Wexler
(Dutton)

Synopsis

This brain teasing collection of close-up things challenges the reader to look with different eyes at things they see daily. The items in each picture are hard to distinguish at first glance, but students identify the items in each picture by using clues to make inferences.

Activity

Select photographs from *Everyday Mysteries*, and prepare clues to accompany each picture, such as *This is something you eat. It has kernels. Sometimes we call it an "ear." What is it?* (corn on the cob) Collect enough film canisters and small items so that you have one canister and item per student. Put a "mystery item" inside each canister. Share the selected photographs with the class, and read the clues. Tell students that making an inference means using clues to make an educated guess. Invite them to make inferences about the pictures based on the clues. Give each student a canister. Tell students to look at their mystery item but to not let anyone else see it. Explain that the class will guess what each student's item is by the clues the student provides. Have students write at least three clues that will help the class determine what their mystery item is. Invite a student to share his or her clues, ask volunteers to guess what the mystery item is, and then ask the student to reveal his or her mystery item to the class. Repeat the activity until every student has shared his or her clues.

Materials

- *Everyday Mysteries*
- empty film canisters
- small items (e.g., seeds, beans, candy)

Test Practice

Give each student a Making Inferences practice test (page 12). Give students 5–10 minutes to complete the test. Review the answers with the entire class.

Name _____   Date _____

Making Inferences

Directions: Read each set of clues. Choose the correct answer.

1. *For Sale:* A large red truck. Comes with a long ladder and siren. Is washed often and can carry several people in special suits and helmets. What is it?

   (a) pickup truck

   (b) school bus

   (c) dump truck

   (d) fire truck

2. *Wanted:* Small house with a door in the front. Will be used in the backyard by a four-legged animal. Must be warm in the winter. If it comes with a bone, that's even better! What is it?

   (a) hamster cage

   (b) doghouse

   (c) barn

   (d) fish tank

3. *Lost:* Metal four-pronged object. Last seen next to a plate. Used daily. Works well with a knife. What is it?

   (a) spoon

   (b) needle

   (c) hammer

   (d) fork

4. Miss Sims is over 5 feet (1.5 meters) tall. Melody is exactly 5 feet (1.5 meters) tall. What inference can you make?

   (a) Miss Sims is taller than Melody.

   (b) Melody is taller than Miss Sims.

   (c) Both women are the same size.

   (d) Miss Sims likes to play basketball.

5. If all boys have yellow and orange spiked hair, and if Brian is a boy, then what else must be true?

   (a) Brian likes to color.

   (b) Brian's favorite color is yellow.

   (c) Brian has yellow and orange spiked hair.

   (d) Brian is smart.

6. The doctor screeched his tires as he wheeled around the corner. He slammed on the brakes and quickly parked his car. He grabbed his medical bag and rushed into the house. What can you infer happened?

   (a) The doctor likes to drive fast.

   (b) He is going to a party.

   (c) It is fun being a doctor.

   (d) Someone inside the house is ill.

Test Prep with a Twist • Gr. 3 © 2003 Creative Teaching Press

Suddenly!

Written by Colin McNaughton
(Harcourt)

Synopsis

Preston the pig, returning home from school, unknowingly has a series of near misses with a lurking wolf. The illustrations show different cliffhangers as Preston does one careful thing after another and averts disaster. The smiling young pig makes it safely home, unaware that he was in any danger.

Activity

Write on separate sentence strips numerous scenarios, such as *I am a dog looking for a bone, I am a cat looking for a mouse,* or *I am a firefighter heading toward a fire.* Draw two columns on a piece of chart paper. Write at the top of the first column *Prediction* and at the top of the second column *Actual.* Read the first page of *Suddenly!* to the class, and have students predict what they think will happen next in the story based on the illustration and their prior knowledge of the topic. Record students' predictions in the "Prediction" column. Turn the first page of the book, and show students if their predictions were correct. Explain that predictions are educated guesses and should be made based on prior experience and one's senses. Record the events from the story in the "Actual" column. Continue to record students' predictions and the actual events. Once you have read the entire book, review the predictions and actual events listed on the chart paper. Divide the class into pairs. Give each pair a sentence strip. Have students read their scenario and think how they could act out their scenario for the class. Allow them 5–10 minutes to prepare their act, and then invite pairs to act out their scenario. After each pair acts out the scenario, have the class infer what the next scene of the scenario may be based on their prior knowledge. Have students record on a piece of paper two things they saw or heard that will help them make a prediction. Remind them that they are using their prior knowledge and their senses to make predictions. Have volunteers share their predictions. Invite the pairs to reveal the actual scenario that they presented.

Materials
- *Suddenly!*
- sentence strips
- chart paper

Test Practice

Give each student a Making Inferences practice test (page 14). Give students 5–10 minutes to complete the test. Review the answers with the entire class.

Name _____   Date _____

Making Inferences

Directions: Review the weather forecast chart. Choose the correct answer for each question.

Five Day Weather Forecast

Sunday	Monday	Tuesday	Wednesday	Thursday
Cloudy with a chance of afternoon showers. Little to no wind expected.	Early morning thunderstorms expected, with light showers continuing throughout the day.	Sunny with warm temperatures all day, and light afternoon breezes. No cloud cover expected.	Cold front approaching by the early afternoon, dropping temperatures by 20 or more degrees.	Warming up today, with high winds and a slight chance of evening showers.

1. You are planning a trip to the lake one late afternoon to do some sailing. Which day should you plan your trip?

   (a) Sunday

   (b) Monday

   (c) Tuesday

   (d) Wednesday

2. Which morning might be the best one to try out your new raincoat and rain boots?

   (a) Sunday

   (b) Monday

   (c) Tuesday

   (d) Wednesday

3. On which day should you **not** take a jacket with you to school?

   (a) Tuesday

   (b) Wednesday

   (c) Thursday

   (d) Friday

4. When will you possibly need an umbrella?

   (a) Monday and Tuesday

   (b) Tuesday and Friday

   (c) Monday and Wednesday

   (d) Sunday, Monday, and Thursday

5. You are planning to test out your new kite one afternoon. When is a good day for this?

   (a) Monday

   (b) Sunday

   (c) Wednesday

   (d) Thursday

6. On which day could you expect to see the sun all day?

   (a) Sunday

   (b) Monday

   (c) Wednesday

   (d) Tuesday

Test Prep with a Twist • Gr. 3 © 2003 Creative Teaching Press

Meanwhile...

Written by Jules Feiffer
(HarperCollins)

Synopsis

Raymond's mother continues to call out his name. To escape her calls, Raymond imagines himself on numerous risky adventures. This unique story uses the word "meanwhile" to change from one scene to the next.

Activity

Bring in the comic strip section of the newspaper. Read *Meanwhile . . .* to the class, and discuss the unique comic book format used by the author. Discuss the importance of sequence in a story and how transition words such as *first, then, next, last,* and *meanwhile* play an important role in leading the reader from event to event. Read a few comic strips to the class. Encourage students to think about the sequence of events in the comics. Record student responses on the board. Tell students that they will create their own comic strip. Brainstorm with the class ideas for comic strip topics. Draw on the board how to create a comic strip by placing captions in boxes. Encourage students to use sequence words when they write. Give each student a What's the Comic? reproducible and an envelope. Have students create their own comic strip, cut out the boxes, place the pieces in an envelope, and write their name on the envelope. Collect the envelopes, and redistribute them. Invite students to read the comic strip pieces and put them in order. Continue to redistribute the envelopes as time permits. Return the envelopes to the original students, and have them glue their comic strip onto a piece of construction paper. Ask volunteers to tell you more sequence words that might have been found in their comic strip, and add the new words to the list on the board.

Materials

- *Meanwhile . . .*
- What's the Comic? reproducible (page 16)
- comic strips
- envelopes
- scissors
- glue
- construction paper

Test Practice

Give each student a Sequencing practice test (page 17). Give students 5–10 minutes to complete the test. Review the answers with the entire class.

What's the Comic?

Test Prep with a Twist · Gr. 3 © 2003 Creative Teaching Press

Name _____   Date _____

Sequencing

Ingredients
2 cups peanut butter chips
5 cups crushed cornflakes
1 tablespoon shortening
1 cup raisins

Peanut Butter Chip Cookies

Directions
Melt the chips and shortening. Stir until smooth and creamy. Combine the cereal, melted chips, and raisins. Stir until the cereal is coated. Drop by spoonfuls onto cookie sheet lined with waxed paper. Chill 1 hour.

Directions: Read the recipe. Answer the questions.

1. In the directions, the **first** step is to

_____.

ⓐ drop by spoonfuls onto waxed paper

ⓑ stir the peanut butter

ⓒ melt the chips and shortening

ⓓ combine the cereal, melted chips, and raisins

2. Which step comes **before** you combine the cereal, melted chips, and raisins?

ⓐ Stir until smooth and creamy.

ⓑ Chill 1 hour.

ⓒ Heat the oven.

ⓓ Stir until the cereal is coated.

3. What are the **last** two ingredients listed in the ingredients list?

ⓐ 5 cups crushed cornflakes and 2 cups peanut butter chips

ⓑ 1 tablespoon shortening and 1 cup raisins

ⓒ 5 cups crushed cornflakes and 1 cup raisins

ⓓ 2 cups peanut butter chips and 1 tablespoon shortening

4. Which step comes **after** you drop the dough by spoonfuls onto a cookie sheet lined with waxed paper?

ⓐ Cook for 10 minutes.

ⓑ Eat and enjoy.

ⓒ Melt chips and shortening.

ⓓ Chill 1 hour.

5. What is the **last** ingredient the directions tell you to add?

ⓐ shortening

ⓑ cornflakes

ⓒ peanut butter chips

ⓓ raisins

6. The **second** ingredient on the list is

_____.

ⓐ raisins

ⓑ cornflakes

ⓒ shortening

ⓓ sugar

Test Prep with a Twist • Gr. 3 © 2003 Creative Teaching Press

The Napping House

Written by Audrey Wood
Illustrated by Don Wood
(Red Wagon Press)

Synopsis

In this cumulative tale, a wakeful flea atop a number of sleeping creatures causes a commotion with just one bite. Because of the way this story is told, it is a great tool to teach sequencing.

Activity

Invite a volunteer to describe to the class the steps for tying a shoelace. As the student describes the steps, write on the board the sequence words that the student uses, such as *first, then, next,* and *finally.* Discuss with the class other terms that could be used when writing the sequence of something, and add those words to the list on the board. Read aloud *The Napping House.* Explain to students that they will take notes about the sequence of the story as you reread the story. Review note-taking strategies. Tell students that they will re-create the sequence of the story based on their notes. Reread the book to the class. Divide the class into pairs. Give each pair a hole punch, several index cards, and yarn. Have partners record each event from the story on an index card. As an option, invite students to illustrate the back of each index card. Then, have students punch a hole in the top and bottom of the appropriate cards. Have them use the yarn to tie the cards together in sequence to create a flow-chart of the story's events. Invite pairs to share their completed flowchart.

Materials
- *The Napping House*
- hole punches
- index cards
- yarn
- crayons or markers (optional)

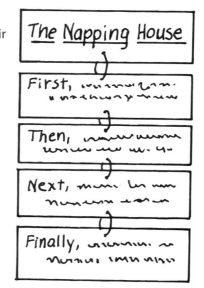

Test Practice

Give each student a Sequencing practice test (page 19). Give students 5–10 minutes to complete the test. Review the answers with the entire class.

Name _____   Date _____

Sequencing

Directions: Read each question, and choose the correct answer.

1. Which of the following is **not** a sequencing word?

    (a) though

    (b) next

    (c) then

    (d) first

2. Read the chart below. It shows the steps to make a bowl of cereal.

First, get a spoon and bowl.
Next, pour the milk.
Finally, eat it!

    What step goes in the empty box?

    (a) Then, wash the bowl.

    (b) Then, clean the table.

    (c) Then, fill the bowl with cereal.

    (d) Then, invite a friend over.

3. To write a letter: first, get a pencil; second, get some paper; _____; then, put it in an envelope; and finally, address the envelope and mail it.

    (a) next, place a stamp on the paper

    (b) next, write the letter

    (c) next, get a drink of water

    (d) next, sharpen the pencil

4. Which of the following words **is** a sequencing word?

    (a) not

    (b) through

    (c) into

    (d) finally

5. To take a photograph of a flower: _____; then, aim the camera at the flower; and finally, push the button to take the picture.

    (a) first, get a camera

    (b) first, get some batteries

    (c) first, get some crayons

    (d) first, take your dog for a walk

6. To brush your teeth: first, get a toothbrush; next, squeeze toothpaste onto the toothbrush; then, wet the toothbrush; and finally, _____.

    (a) wash your hands

    (b) brush your teeth

    (c) comb your hair

    (d) get in the shower

Comprehension

Test Prep with a Twist · Gr. 3 © 2003 Creative Teaching Press

Cowboy Sam and Those Confounded Secrets

Written by Kitty Griffin and Kathy Combs
(Clarion Books)

Synopsis

Cowboy Sam, the biggest secret keeper in the town, is able to keep any secret under his 10-gallon hat. A problem arises when Cowboy Sam's hat is filled past capacity and the secrets begin to leak out. Cowboy Sam becomes really sad when he realizes that he has let the town down. He soon discovers a new place to hide his secrets where they won't leak out.

Activity

Read to the class *Cowboy Sam and Those Confounded Secrets* without showing the illustrations. Then, explain to the class that they will create a picture of where the story takes place. Give each student a piece of drawing paper, and invite students to draw, color, or paint a picture of their impression of where the story took place. Invite students to share their picture. Have them observe what each picture has in common. Discuss how students came up with the setting of the story without seeing the original illustrations from the book. Point out how certain words help to explain the setting of the story. Reread the story, and show the illustrations. Have students locate the words that help describe the setting. Record student responses on the board. For example, students might say *armadillo, longhorn, Texas drawl, chili peppers,* and *Cowboy Sam.* To extend the activity, have them write and illustrate a class story similar to *Cowboy Sam and Those Confounded Secrets* but with a new setting, such as *Arctic Sam.*

Materials

- *Cowboy Sam and Those Confounded Secrets*
- drawing paper
- crayons or markers or paint/paintbrushes

Kendall

Test Practice

Give each student a Setting practice test (page 21). Give students 5–10 minutes to complete the test. Review the answers with the entire class.

Name _____   Date _____

Setting

Directions: Choose the correct answer for each question.

1. Since school is out, the children are splashing and swimming in the neighborhood pool. What season is it?

    (a) fall

    (b) winter

    (c) spring

    (d) summer

2. The small child tries to keep his eyes closed, but the sun begins to shine through his window. What time of day is it?

    (a) evening

    (b) dawn

    (c) afternoon

    (d) dusk

3. I hear a rooster crowing and cows mooing as I step outside. Where am I?

    (a) by the ocean

    (b) in the city

    (c) on a farm

    (d) in a school

4. The little girl yawns and stretches as she rolls out of bed to get ready for school. What time of day is it?

    (a) morning

    (b) night

    (c) afternoon

    (d) evening

5. The snow skiers race toward the finish line. Where are they?

    (a) in the ocean

    (b) on a mountain

    (c) in the desert

    (d) in the rain forest

6. As the children walk through the park, they notice how the leaves are changing into beautiful colors of red and gold. What season is it?

    (a) spring

    (b) summer

    (c) fall

    (d) winter

7. The children eat cotton candy and watch the clowns do tricks. Where were they?

    (a) on a farm

    (b) at the zoo

    (c) at the circus

    (d) in a swimming pool

8. The boy and his father saw many animals. Their favorite animal was the lion. Where were they?

    (a) in the desert

    (b) at the zoo

    (c) at the beach

    (d) at an amusement park

Aunt Isabel Tells a Good One

Written by Kate Duke
(Dutton)

Synopsis

As Aunt Isabel, a bohemian-looking mouse, tells little Penelope a story, Penelope discovers what it takes to make a story good. This story illustrates the importance of using specific literary elements within fictional stories to convey the story's meaning.

Activity

Copy the Story Map onto an overhead transparency. Read *Aunt Isabel Tells a Good One* to the class, and tell students to think about what elements make this story so interesting and easy to understand. Display the transparency. Review the meaning of each story element. For example, the setting is when and where the story takes place. Ask volunteers to share the elements from the story. Write student responses on the story map. Write each story element listed on the transparency at the top of a separate piece of butcher paper. Divide the class into six groups, and give each group a piece of butcher paper. Explain that groups will write a short definition of their story element and draw a picture or create a short chant or song to help explain it. For example, for setting students could write *The setting means where and when the story takes place*. Students could then draw examples of settings that represent where (e.g., forest, school, ocean) and when (e.g., summer, Christmas, Father's Day, midnight). Invite groups to present their definition and display their drawing or recite their chant or song. Then, invite volunteers to review the definitions of all the story elements.

Materials

- *Aunt Isabel Tells a Good One*
- Story Map (page 23)
- overhead projector/ transparency
- butcher paper
- crayons or markers

The setting means where and when the story takes place.

Test Practice

Read a well-known version of Cinderella to the class. Give each student a Story Elements practice test (page 24). Give students 5–10 minutes to complete the test. Review the answers with the entire class.

Story Map

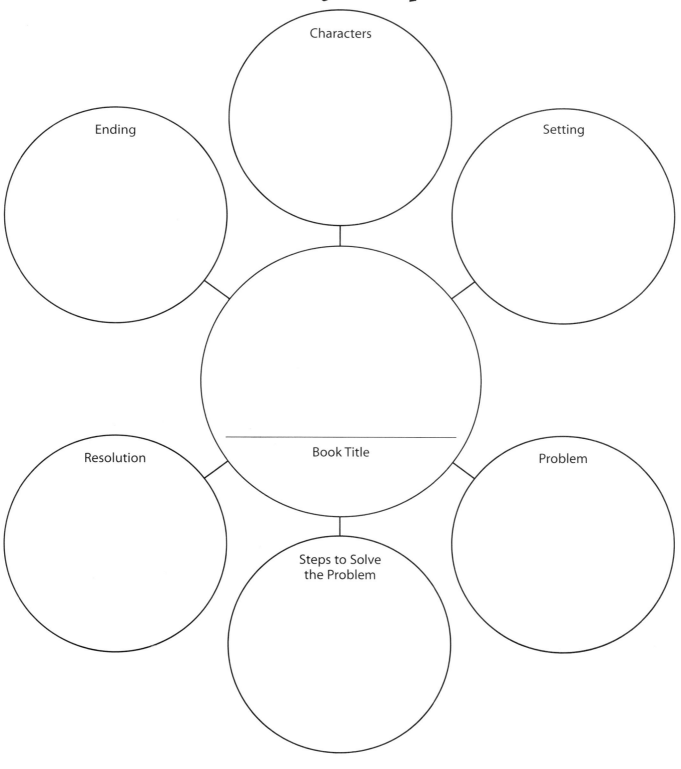

Characters

Ending

Setting

Book Title

Resolution

Problem

Steps to Solve
the Problem

Name _____   Date _____

Story Elements

Directions: Read each sentence. Choose the answer that best completes each sentence about the story of Cinderella.

1. The main character is ...
   - (a) the fairy godmother.
   - (b) the Prince.
   - (c) Cinderella.
   - (d) the ugly stepsisters.

2. The setting of the story is ...
   - (a) long ago in the Prince's kingdom.
   - (b) springtime in England.
   - (c) winter at the fairy godmother's house.
   - (d) Christmastime at Cinderella's house.

3. The main problem is ...
   - (a) Cinderella cannot go to the ball.
   - (b) the clock struck six.
   - (c) Cinderella lost her tiny glass slipper when she ran away from the Prince.
   - (d) Cinderella's father was poor.

4. One of the steps to solve the problem is ...
   - (a) the stepsisters are mean to Cinderella.
   - (b) the fairy godmother turns the pumpkin into a carriage.
   - (c) the clock struck twelve.
   - (d) the Prince tries the glass slipper on the feet of Cinderella's stepsisters.

5. The resolution of the story is ...
   - (a) the stepsisters try on the glass slipper.
   - (b) Cinderella tries on the glass slipper, and it fits her foot perfectly.
   - (c) the fairy godmother makes beautiful clothes for Cinderella to wear to the ball.
   - (d) when Cinderella returns from the ball, she is again dressed in rags.

6. The ending of the story is ...
   - (a) Cinderella marries the Prince.
   - (b) the stepsisters never forgive Cinderella for marrying the Prince.
   - (c) the glass slipper breaks at Cinderella's wedding.
   - (d) the fairy godmother disappeared.

7. How would you describe Cinderella at the end of the story?
   - (a) Cinderella is sad to be on her own.
   - (b) Cinderella is happy she is with the Prince.
   - (c) Cinderella is lonely for her stepsisters.
   - (d) Cinderella is wishing she could clean the house again.

8. The word that **best** describes Cinderella is ...
   - (a) unkind
   - (b) disrespectful
   - (c) indifferent
   - (d) respectful

Test Prep with a Twist • Gr. 3 © 2003 Creative Teaching Press

Toad

Written by Ruth Brown
(Puffin)

Synopsis

Ruth Brown's colorful, vivid language paints a detailed picture of the toad, who survives an encounter with a desperately hungry monster and lives to crunch, munch, and slurp more bugs!

Activity

Have students close their eyes as you read aloud *Toad*. Discuss the mental pictures students created. Read the story again, and show the pictures. Ask students *How was your mental picture of Toad similar to or different from the author's picture?* Invite volunteers to share their findings. Give each student a Pet Advertisement reproducible, and challenge students to rewrite the ad using numerous adjectives to make it more descriptive. For example, a student may write *Cute, cuddly kitten! Free to good home. Soft, fluffy, white, adorable. Perfect for playful children and loving family.* Invite volunteers to share their advertisement with the class.

Materials
• *Toad*
• Pet Advertisement reproducible (page 26)

CLASSIFIEDS

Cute, cuddly kitten!

Free to good home.
Soft, fluffy,
white, adorable.

Test Practice

Give each student an Adjectives practice test (page 27). Give students 5–10 minutes to complete the test. Review the answers with the entire class.

Pet Advertisement

Directions: Rewrite the advertisement using numerous adjectives to help persuade someone to buy your kitten.

Free kitten. Nice to play with. Please take.

CLASSIFIEDS

_____

_____

_____

_____

_____

_____

_____

Test Prep with a Twist • Gr. 3 © 2003 Creative Teaching Press

Name _____   Date _____

Adjectives

Directions: Find the adjective in each sentence.

1. The cheerful children skipped home from school today.
   - (a) children
   - (b) skipped
   - (c) school
   - (d) cheerful

2. Horses galloped wildly in the enormous pasture.
   - (a) galloped
   - (b) wildly
   - (c) enormous
   - (d) horses

3. The hungry rabbits ate carrots and cucumbers from the garden.
   - (a) rabbits
   - (b) carrots
   - (c) hungry
   - (d) ate

4. The dog's noisy barking woke the baby.
   - (a) woke
   - (b) noisy
   - (c) barking
   - (d) baby

5. The creepy spiders scaled the pipe outside.
   - (a) pipe
   - (b) creepy
   - (c) scaled
   - (d) spiders

6. The nervous puppy paced back and forth across the floor.
   - (a) nervous
   - (b) puppy
   - (c) floor
   - (d) paced

7. Curious kittens climbed the tree to get a look at the nest.
   - (a) tree
   - (b) nest
   - (c) climbed
   - (d) Curious

8. The beautiful ballerina curtsied after her performance.
   - (a) curtsied
   - (b) beautiful
   - (c) after
   - (d) ballerina

Things That Are Most in the World

Written by Judi Barrett
Illustrated by John Nickle
(Aladdin)

Synopsis

The lively illustrations and clever humor that abound in this book expose the reader to the silliest, prickliest, smelliest, and teensie-weensiest things in the world!

Activity

Discuss with the class the rules for adding *-er* and *-est* to adjectives. Explain that comparative adjectives compare two things and end with *-er* and superlative adjectives compare three or more things and end with *-est*. Demonstrate this concept by comparing two and then three students' heights. For example, say *Brett is tall, Abby is taller than Brett, and Allison is tallest of all*. Make additional comparisons between lines drawn on the chalkboard—long, longer, longest, or short, shorter, and shortest. Read *Things That Are Most in the World* to the class. Point out the use of exaggeration in both the pictures and text. Have students brainstorm a list of superlative adjectives. Record student responses on the board. Model how to write an exaggeration with a superlative. For example, choose the word *smelliest*, and write *The smelliest thing in the world is a pair of socks that have been worn for three months and are now at the bottom of a trashcan*. Invite each student to select a different adjective from the board. Give each student a piece of drawing paper, and invite students to write and illustrate an exaggerated sentence with the adjective they chose. Invite volunteers to share their sentence. Collect students' papers, and bind them together to create a class book titled *Things That Are Most*.

Materials

- *Things That Are Most in the World*
- drawing paper
- crayons or markers
- bookbinding materials

Test Practice

Give each student an Adjectives: Superlatives practice test (page 29). Give students 5–10 minutes to complete the test. Review the answers with the entire class.

Adjectives: Superlatives

Directions: Find the adjective that best completes each sentence.

1. The _____ clown wore red and white stripes.
   - (a) colder
   - (b) silliest
   - (c) darker
   - (d) darkest

2. The _____ bottlenose dolphin jumped the highest.
   - (a) weakest
   - (b) slower
   - (c) bravest
   - (d) slowest

3. The _____ runner won the race.
   - (a) fastest
   - (b) slower
   - (c) slowest
   - (d) faster

4. The planet Pluto is _____ away from the sun.
   - (a) far
   - (b) farthest
   - (c) farther
   - (d) nicest

5. Darrell is the _____ basketball player on the team.
   - (a) tall
   - (b) taller
   - (c) easiest
   - (d) tallest

6. Sally was the _____ girl in the school.
   - (a) friendliest
   - (b) friendlier
   - (c) longest
   - (d) hardest

7. That cactus was the _____ one she grew.
   - (a) prickliest
   - (b) dirtiest
   - (c) slowest
   - (d) meanest

8. Bob's chili was the _____ chili in the contest.
   - (a) loudest
   - (b) shortest
   - (c) lowest
   - (d) hottest

Test Prep with a Twist • Gr. 3 © 2003 Creative Teaching Press

Amelia and Eleanor Go for a Ride

Written by Pam Munoz Ryan
Illustrated by Brian Selznick
(Scholastic)

Synopsis

This book is the fictionalized account of the night Amelia Earhart flew Eleanor Roosevelt over Washington, D.C., in an airplane. The author conducted extensive research to include documented conversations between these two historical figures.

Activity

Review with the class the definition of a proper noun. Remind students that a proper noun is the name of one specific person or place. Ask volunteers to provide examples of proper nouns. Record student responses on the board. Read aloud *Amelia and Eleanor Go for a Ride*, and pause to write on the board the proper nouns found in the book. Review the list of words on the board, and invite volunteers to underline the capital letter in each word. Divide the class into small groups. Explain to students that they will write riddles that describe famous places or landmarks. For example, students could write *I am a famous landmark located in a mountain in North Dakota. There are four presidents carved in me. What famous landmark am I?* Have students write several riddles. Invite groups to share their riddles with the class.

Materials

• *Amelia and Eleanor Go for a Ride*

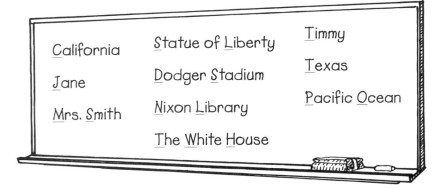

California   Statue of Liberty   Timmy
Jane   Dodger Stadium   Texas
Mrs. Smith   Nixon Library   Pacific Ocean
              The White House

Test Practice

Give each student a Capitalization of Proper Nouns practice test (page 31). Give students 5–10 minutes to complete the test. Review the answers with the entire class.

Capitalization of Proper Nouns

Directions: Read each story. Find the line with the capitalization mistake.

1. **line one:**   On saturday, my sister went for a ride
   line two: in her new convertible. Since it was a
   line three: gorgeous day, she put down the top.

   (a) line one
   (b) line two
   (c) line three
   (d) no mistake

2. **line one:**   Have you ever been fishing for
   line two: large fish? i spent a week last
   line three: month at the seashore.

   (a) line one
   (b) line two
   (c) line three
   (d) no mistake

3. **line one:**   The people could not believe their
   line two: eyes when they arrived at sandy zoo.
   line three: The monkeys were playing a game.

   (a) line one
   (b) line two
   (c) line three
   (d) no mistake

4. **line one:**   Mrs. Dodd had a large celebration
   line two: for the 4th of July. Everyone
   line three: from her neighborhood was there.

   (a) line one
   (b) line two
   (c) line three
   (d) no mistake

5. **line one:**   My friend has a valuable baseball
   line two: card collection. His favorite card
   line three: is the one signed by babe ruth.

   (a) line one
   (b) line two
   (c) line three
   (d) no mistake

6. **line one:**   When the talented artist strolled
   line two: along the streets of paris, she was
   line three: shocked by the number of people.

   (a) line one
   (b) line two
   (c) line three
   (d) no mistake

Test Prep with a Twist • Gr. 3 © 2003 Creative Teaching Press

The Teacher from the Black Lagoon

Written by Mike Thaler
Illustrated by Jared Lee
(Scholastic)

Synopsis

A little boy's biggest fears come true as he arrives at school for his first day and wonders what his new teacher will be like. He discovers that his teacher is really a monster with a tail and has smoke coming out of her nostrils! Fortunately, the little boy is only dreaming and when he wakes up he realizes his teacher, Mrs. Green, is the wonderful teacher he had hoped for.

Activity

Read *The Teacher from the Black Lagoon* to the class, and discuss what contractions are. Reread sentences from the story that contain contractions, and invite students to raise their hand when they hear a contraction. Record on the board student responses as well as the two words that each contraction represents. For example, write *couldn't—could not*. Divide the class into pairs. Tell students that they will go on a "contraction scavenger hunt." Explain that their goal is to look through classroom books, magazines, and newspapers to find as many contractions as they can. Have pairs record their contractions on a piece of paper. After students complete their scavenger hunt, invite them to share some of their contractions. Record student responses on the board. Give each pair numerous index cards in two different colors. Have students write each contraction on one colored card and the two words that each contraction represents on the other colored card. For example, if students have green and blue index cards, they might write *can't* on the green card and *cannot* on the blue card. Ask pairs to mix up their cards and place them facedown in rows on a desk or the floor for a game of Concentration. Have players take turns turning over one of each colored card. If a student selects a contraction and its match, he or she keeps the cards and gets another turn. If the student does not select a match, have the student place the cards facedown in the original location, and the other player gets a turn. Once students have collected all the cards, have them count their cards. The player with the most cards wins.

Materials
- *The Teacher from the Black Lagoon*
- index cards in 2 colors

Test Practice

Give each student a Contractions practice test (page 33). Give students 5–10 minutes to complete the test. Review the answers with the entire class.

Name _____   Date _____

Contractions

Directions: Read each sentence. Look at each underlined contraction. Choose the answer that tells which
word or words the contraction represents.

1. I <u>can't</u> wait until my birthday.

   (a) will not

   (b) should not

   (c) cannot

   (d) could not

2. <u>You've</u> been playing for two hours.

   (a) you are

   (b) you have

   (c) you is

   (d) you been

3. We <u>shouldn't</u> run in the house.

   (a) should not

   (b) should no

   (c) should have

   (d) should is

4. <u>We've</u> been on a long vacation.

   (a) we are

   (b) we am

   (c) we have

   (d) we has

5. My dog <u>doesn't</u> smell very well.

   (a) do not

   (b) does not

   (c) dare not

   (d) will not

6. <u>That's</u> my ice cream.

   (a) that have

   (b) that are

   (c) that is

   (d) that were

7. I <u>don't</u> want to ride my bike today.

   (a) do now

   (b) does not

   (c) does have

   (d) do not

8. <u>I'm</u> making a cake for my mom.

   (a) I have

   (b) I was

   (c) I are

   (d) I am

Test Prep with a Twist • Gr. 3 © 2003 Creative Teaching Press

Puppy Riddles

Written by Katy Hall and Lisa Eisenberg
Illustrated by Thor Wickstrom
(Penguin Putnam)

Synopsis

Puppy Riddles is a collection of forty-two riddles that deal with adorable pets in all kinds of "puppy situations." This is a good book to reinforce statements and questions with a topic that will appeal to all students!

Activity

Read *Puppy Riddles* to the class, and draw students' attention to the type of punctuation used at the end of each sentence. Students should notice that each riddle starts by asking a question (interrogative sentence) and ends with a statement (declarative sentence). Explain that interrogative sentences end with a question mark and declarative sentences end with a period. For example, say *How do we know puppies like their dads? They always lick their paws.* Give each student a Riddle Strip reproducible. Have students write on the first strip the question part of the riddle without the question mark, and have them write on the second strip the statement part of the riddle without the period. Have them cut apart their completed strips. Collect the question strips and statement strips separately, mix them up, and redistribute one of each strip to each student. Have each student read the two strips and determine which is a question and which is a statement. Give each student a marker, and invite students to add a question mark or a period to the appropriate sentences. Invite each student to read aloud his or question. Ask the student with the riddle's answer to stand and read the statement to the class. Continue the activity until all students have had a turn to read both their sentence strips.

Materials
- *Puppy Riddles*
- Riddle Strip reproducible (page 35)
- scissors
- colored markers

> How do we
> know puppies
> like their dads

> They always
> lick their
> paws

Test Practice

Give each student a copy of the Periods and Question Marks practice test (page 36). Give students 5–10 minutes to complete the test. Review the answers with the entire class.

Riddle Strip

Directions: Write the question part of your riddle in the first box. Do not add the question mark. Write the statement part of your riddle in the second box. Do not add the period. Cut around both boxes.

Ah! Ha! Ha!

Ha! Ha! Ha!

Hee-Hee-Hee

Test Prep with a Twist • Gr. 3 © 2003 Creative Teaching Press

Periods and Question Marks

Directions: Read each question. Choose the sentence that needs a period or a question mark.

1. Which sentence needs a **period**?

   ⓐ Should I always tell the truth

   ⓑ Taylor hit a home run in the game

   ⓒ When does the movie start

   ⓓ What would you like for dinner

2. Which sentence needs a **question mark**?

   ⓐ It rained hard last night

   ⓑ We had a substitute teacher today

   ⓒ Where are my new shoes

   ⓓ My dog's name is Tucker

3. Which sentence needs a **period**?

   ⓐ Have you ever read *Charlotte's Web*

   ⓑ Do horses gallop quickly

   ⓒ How is Aunt Martha

   ⓓ David mowed the lawn yesterday

4. Which sentence needs a **question mark**?

   ⓐ Who ate the last cookie

   ⓑ Alaska is a beautiful state

   ⓒ The Wright Brothers were famous pilots

   ⓓ Soccer is a tough sport

5. Which sentence needs a **period**?

   ⓐ Can you help with homework

   ⓑ The spaghetti is delicious

   ⓒ Why is the sky blue

   ⓓ How is the car running

6. Which sentence needs a **question mark**?

   ⓐ The car is nice and clean now

   ⓑ Justin is a math whiz

   ⓒ Did you make your bed

   ⓓ Please eat your green beans

7. Which sentence needs a **period**?

   ⓐ People love to laugh at jokes

   ⓑ What time is breakfast, Mom

   ⓒ Would you stop tickling me

   ⓓ May I have some more ice cream

8. Which sentence needs a **question mark**?

   ⓐ Matthew dropped the ball

   ⓑ The lightbulb was a great invention

   ⓒ Isn't America a wonderful place to live

   ⓓ Bring me the nails

In the Small, Small Pond

Written and illustrated by Denise Fleming
(Scholastic)

Synopsis

Verbs abound in this pond filled with animals splashing, swooping, lunging, and wiggling! This unique book about animal life introduces habitats and the change of seasons.

Activity

Review with the class the definition of a verb. Explain to students that verbs are action words. Read *In the Small, Small Pond* to the class, and ask volunteers to share some of the verbs they heard in the story. Record student responses on the board. Have students brainstorm additional verbs that apply to the classroom setting. For example, students might say *write, paint,* and *read.* Record these words on the board. Give each student or pair of students a thesaurus. Encourage students to use the thesaurus to help them find alternate words to replace the more common verbs listed on the board. For example, they could replace *write* with *compose, scrawl,* or *scribe.* Challenge students to create a page for a class book titled *In the Busy, Busy Classroom.* For example, students could write *In the busy, busy class-room, Susie composes, converses, and sketches.* Encourage them to create an illustration that depicts one or more of their verbs. Invite volunteers to share their paper with the class. Collect the papers, and bind them together to create a class book.

Materials

- *In the Small, Small Pond*
- thesauruses
- crayons or markers
- bookbinding materials

In the busy, busy classroom, Susie composes, converses, and sketches.

Test Practice

Give each student a Verbs practice test (page 38). Give students 5–10 minutes to complete the test. Review the answers with the entire class.

Name _____   Date _____

Verbs

Directions: Find the verb in each sentence.

1. The horse galloped through the grassy meadow.
   - (a) horse
   - (b) galloped
   - (c) grassy
   - (d) meadow

2. Children laughed at the circus clown.
   - (a) children
   - (b) clown
   - (c) circus
   - (d) laughed

3. The siren on the police car shrieked.
   - (a) siren
   - (b) police
   - (c) car
   - (d) shrieked

4. The children splashed each other in the pool.
   - (a) children
   - (b) splashed
   - (c) other
   - (d) pool

5. The teachers read enthusiastically to their students.
   - (a) read
   - (b) their
   - (c) teachers
   - (d) students

6. The playful kittens scratched the new table.
   - (a) playful
   - (b) scratched
   - (c) kittens
   - (d) table

7. Daddy mowed the lawn last Saturday.
   - (a) mowed
   - (b) Daddy
   - (c) lawn
   - (d) Saturday

8. Bob and Sue walked to the park on a warm, sunny day.
   - (a) Bob
   - (b) park
   - (c) Sue
   - (d) walked

Test Prep with a Twist • Gr. 3 © 2003 Creative Teaching Press

Over in the Meadow

Written by Ezra Jack Keats
(Puffin)

Synopsis

Children love this classic rhyme that is often used to teach counting. However, older children can learn about verbs in this story that takes place in a lush meadow bustling with activity!

Activity

Review with students the definition of a verb. Explain that a verb tells what the noun does. For example, in the sentence *Noah ran down the street*, *ran* tells what *Noah* did. Tell students to listen for the action words as you read the story. Read aloud *Over in the Meadow*, and discuss the types of animals found in the story and the action of each animal. Record student responses on the board. Ask students to silently read all the action verbs listed on the board and to think about how the verbs vary. Encourage them to notice how the verbs have different tenses. Explain to the class that the spelling of a verb may change depending on if it is in the past, present, or future tense. Give each student a Past, Present, and Future reproducible. Invite students to list each animal from the story in the first column and then list the past, present, and future tenses for the animal's action verb in the appropriate column. For example, for *turtle* students would write animal—*turtle*, past—*dug*, present—*dig*, and future—*will dig*. Complete three or four examples with the class. Provide dictionaries to help students find the spelling of the past tense of irregular verbs.

Materials
- *Over in the Meadow*
- Past, Present, and Future reproducible (page 40)
- dictionaries

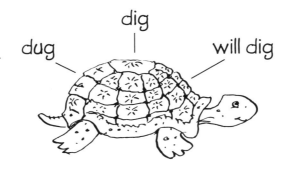

Test Practice

Give each student a Verb Tenses practice test (page 41). Give students 5–10 minutes to complete the test. Review the answers with the entire class.

Past, Present, and Future

Directions: Write the name of each animal from the story in the first column. Write the past, present, and future tenses of the animal's verb in the remaining columns.

Animal Name	Past	Present	Future
turtle	dug	dig	will dig

Test Prep with a Twist · Gr. 3 © 2003 Creative Teaching Press

Name _____ Date _____

Verb Tenses

Directions: Read each sentence carefully. Choose the correct verb tense to complete each sentence.

1. Last summer, Grandpa _____ us a story about when he was a little boy.
   - (a) tell
   - (b) told
   - (c) will tell
   - (d) telling

2. Tomorrow, Susie _____ a picture in her art class.
   - (a) paint
   - (b) painted
   - (c) will paint
   - (d) painting

3. It seems like it was a long time ago when we _____ in the ocean.
   - (a) swim
   - (b) swam
   - (c) will swim
   - (d) swimming

4. The coach taught the little boy how to hit the ball and _____ to first base.
   - (a) run
   - (b) ran
   - (c) will run
   - (d) running

5. The piano player _____ beautifully in the recital last night.
   - (a) play
   - (b) played
   - (c) will play
   - (d) playing

6. Bob is _____ to catch a large fish on his fishing trip.
   - (a) hope
   - (b) hoped
   - (c) will hope
   - (d) hoping

7. Sometimes, tears come out of our eyes when we _____ too hard.
   - (a) laugh
   - (b) laughed
   - (c) will laugh
   - (d) laughing

8. _____ high is something basketball players should do well.
   - (a) Jumper
   - (b) Jumped
   - (c) Will jump
   - (d) Jumping

Test Prep with a Twist · Gr. 3 © 2003 Creative Teaching Press

The Greatest Gymnast of All

Written by Stuart J. Murphy
Illustrated by Cynthia Jabar
(Econo-Clad Books)

Synopsis

Through a series of leaps, swings, and flips, a young girl tumbles her way inside, outside, on, off, near, far, forward, and backward as she works toward becoming a great gymnast.

Activity

Explain to the class that an antonym is a word that means the opposite of something. List examples on the board such as *hot* and *cold* and *dark* and *light*. Read *The Greatest Gymnast of All* to the class, and ask students to name some of the antonyms they heard in the story. Record student responses on the board. Challenge the class to come up with additional antonyms to add to the list so that you have a pair of antonyms for each student. Give each student two index cards. Have students choose a word and its antonym from the board and write the words on their index cards. Erase each pair of words from the board when a student selects it. Write *I have Start* and *Stop* on two additional index cards. Collect the students' cards, and shuffle them together with the two extra cards. Explain to the class that they will play a game called I Have, Who Has? Give each student two word cards, and take two cards for yourself. Invite the student with the "I have Start" card to begin the game by reading both of his or her cards. For example, the student would say *I have Start. Who has the antonym for* **outside?** Then, the student with the antonym for *outside* would say *I have* **inside.** *Who has the antonym for* **sour?** Continue the game until all students have a chance to read their cards.

Materials
- *The Greatest Gymnast of All*
- index cards

black–white	hot–cold
happy–sad	give–take
tall–short	rich–poor
nice–mean	high–low

hot cold

Test Practice

Give each student an Antonyms practice test (page 43). Give students 5–10 minutes to complete the test. Review the answers with the entire class.

Name _____ Date _____

Antonyms

Directions: Read each sentence. Choose the antonym (opposite) of each underlined word.

1. The baby cried <u>loudly</u> for her mother.
   - (a) quickly
   - (b) noisily
   - (c) quietly
   - (d) happily

2. The <u>warm</u> weather was perfect for a day at the lake.
   - (a) hot
   - (b) cool
   - (c) sunny
   - (d) rainy

3. The high school football game was a <u>lengthy</u> one.
   - (a) short
   - (b) good
   - (c) long
   - (d) wide

4. Airplanes fly <u>over</u> our house all day and night.
   - (a) above
   - (b) around
   - (c) outside
   - (d) under

5. The mountain was <u>full</u> of skiers and spectators.
   - (a) filled
   - (b) packed
   - (c) empty
   - (d) busy

6. The first snow brought <u>chilly</u> temperatures.
   - (a) warm
   - (b) cool
   - (c) pretty
   - (d) icy

7. Limousines pulled <u>forward</u> to pick up the musicians.
   - (a) ahead
   - (b) backward
   - (c) below
   - (d) around

8. Seven <u>strong</u> men loaded the angry elephant into the truck.
   - (a) tough
   - (b) large
   - (c) kind
   - (d) weak

Vocabulary

That's Not Fair, Hare!

Written by Julie Sykes
(Penguin)

Synopsis

The turtle and the hare are back again, but this version of the story has surprises and laughs that aren't in the original. The race is on and the fun begins! Muggs the turtle gives her best effort, but turtles aren't designed for speed. Worse yet, Greedy Hare has a couple of sly tricks up his sleeve.

Activity

Write the following sentences on the board:

One day, Muggs the turtle plodded down to the farmer's cabbage field for lunch.

Greedy Hare zoomed off, shouting rudely, "See you tomorrow Muggs, or will it be next week?"

Squirrel cheerfully scampered along, giving Muggs kind words of encouragement.

Quickly he scrambled to his paws.

Muggs overtook Greedy Hare just before she reached the field.

Muggs crept quietly past the sleeping hare and over the bridge.

Materials

- *That's Not Fair, Hare!*
- blank paper
- construction paper
- stapler
- crayons or markers

Prepare a mini-book for each student by placing seven blank pages between a piece of folded construction paper and stapling the book on the fold. Read *That's Not Fair, Hare!* to the class, and draw students' attention to the challenging vocabulary words, such as *plodded, scampered,* and *overtook*. Explain how the context in which a word is found and the pictures help clarify the meaning of difficult words. Invite volunteers to read the sentences aloud. Give each student a prepared mini-book. Have students write the underlined words from the board on separate pages. Have them use the clues in the story's pictures and text to create and illustrate their own definition for each word. Invite volunteers to share their completed book.

Test Practice

Give each student a Context Clues practice test (page 45). Give students 5–10 minutes to complete the test. Review the answers with the entire class.

Name _____   Date _____

Context Clues

Directions: Choose the correct word to replace the underlined word in each sentence.

1. The <u>greedy</u> little girl took all of the candy for herself and did not share.

   (a) nice
   (b) selfish
   (c) sleepy
   (d) happy

2. The children went around and around on the <u>carousel</u> at the fair.

   (a) merry-go-round
   (b) radio
   (c) balloons
   (d) slide

3. The campers floated down the river in their <u>kayak</u>.

   (a) car
   (b) canoe
   (c) bike
   (d) tent

4. The <u>sluggish</u> turtle laid down in the sand after a long walk.

   (a) quick
   (b) hungry
   (c) happy
   (d) slow

5. The young boy <u>taunted</u> the puppy by holding a bone in front of the puppy's nose.

   (a) flipped
   (b) colored
   (c) teased
   (d) sneezed

6. We <u>trudged</u> up the hill through the mud and rain.

   (a) swam
   (b) ate
   (c) danced
   (d) walked tiredly

7. The hungry bear <u>devoured</u> all the berries in the picnic basket.

   (a) hid
   (b) ate
   (c) cooked
   (d) roared

8. The soccer team gave their best <u>effort</u> to win the game.

   (a) try
   (b) look
   (c) guess
   (d) time

Vocabulary

Test Prep with a Twist • Gr. 3 © 2003 Creative Teaching Press

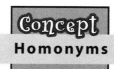
The King Who Rained

Written by Fred Gwynne
(Aladdin)

Synopsis

A little girl uses her imagination to come up with pictures of things that her parents are talking about. The little girl visualizes a bear's feet when her parents discuss "bear feet." This book uses homonyms and makes a game of them as seen from a child's understanding of the English language.

Activity

Copy the Homonym Search reproducible onto an overhead transparency. Select from *The King Who Rained* several pages you feel would be difficult for students to understand. Read aloud the first page you chose, and ask students what they noticed about the text and illustration. They should notice that the homonyms are used incorrectly. Display the transparency, and read the definition of a homonym to the class. As you read each selected page from the book, record in the appropriate column the homonym used in the text and the correct homonym, which should make the statement true. Ask volunteers to tell you the meaning of each word, and record the meaning underneath the word. Give each student a piece of construction paper. Have students fold their paper widthwise and then reopen it. Invite students to select a homonym pair from the transparency and write the first homonym at the bottom of the first column and the second homonym at the bottom of the second column. Invite students to draw above each homonym a picture that describes the homonym correctly. For example, a student might select the homonym pair *ate* and *eight* and draw a child eating an apple in the first column and a child holding up eight fingers in the second column. Have volunteers share their completed paper.

Materials
- *The King Who Rained*
- Homonym Search reproducible (page 47)
- overhead projector/transparency
- 9" x 12" (23 cm x 30.5 cm) construction paper

Test Practice

Give each student a Homonyms practice test (page 48). Give students 5–10 minutes to complete the test. Review the answers with the entire class.

Name _____ Date _____

Homonym Search

Homonyms are two or more words that are pronounced the same but have different meanings. For example, *to, too,* and *two* are homonyms.

Homonym Used in Context	Matching Homonym

Vocabulary

Test Prep with a Twist · Gr. 3 © 2003 Creative Teaching Press

Homonyms

Directions: Read each sentence. Choose the correct definition for each underlined homonym.

1. The knight will only wear his armor at <u>night</u>.
   a) warrior that fights on horseback
   b) a king
   c) when it is light
   d) the time between sunset and sunrise

2. The nurse's <u>aide</u> gives first aid to injured children in our school.
   a) a donation given to the needy
   b) a helper
   c) a teacher
   d) a present

3. If a baseball hits you, try not to <u>bawl</u>.
   a) run
   b) duck
   c) cry
   d) laugh

4. The fisherman and his <u>peer</u> met at the pier at dawn to do some fishing.
   a) an equal person
   b) to look at closely
   c) a landing place for boats
   d) a ship's captain

5. The boy took the horse's <u>reins</u> and led it into the stall before the rain started.
   a) an animal's head
   b) straps used to control an animal
   c) to rule
   d) water that falls from the sky

6. We heard the applause as the <u>herd</u> of elephants entered the circus ring.
   a) to sense sounds
   b) group of animals
   c) to see things
   d) kind of animal

7. It is not fair to charge a large <u>fare</u> to enter the County Fair.
   a) the cost of something
   b) an outdoor show of farm animals
   c) reasonable treatment
   d) light in color

8. You will not be able to get your shoes off if the shoelaces have <u>knots</u> in them.
   a) at no time
   b) the speed of a ship
   c) a hard spot in wood
   d) string fastened together with loops

See the Yak Yak

Written by Charles Ghigna
Illustrated by Brian Lies
(Random House)

Synopsis

Comical illustrations help readers see unbelievable things such as *a fly fly, a yak yak,* or *a duck duck.* Readers will learn about homonyms as they decode the simple text.

Activity

Ask students to close their eyes and visualize the sentence *The man in the field caught a fly.* Ask volunteers to describe what they see when they hear the sentence. Some students may see a baseball player catching a ball, while others may think the sentence is about an insect. Discuss the importance of using context clues to determine the meanings of words. Read *See the Yak Yak* to the class without showing the pictures. Discuss the multiple meanings of specific words in the story as you read each page. After you finish the story, show the class the illustrations. Invite volunteers to tell you words with multiple meanings from the story and any additional words they know. Record student responses on the board. Invite students to select a word from the book and write a sentence that follows the format of the story. Each sentence should include both meanings of the word. Some examples might include *Did you see the fly fly? Can a swallow swallow? Did you hear the creek creak?* or *I wonder if a watch can watch.* Have students draw a picture that depicts both definitions of the word. Invite them to share their completed work with the class. Collect students' papers, and bind them together to create a class book.

Materials
- *See the Yak Yak*
- crayons or markers
- bookbinding materials

Test Practice

Give each student a Multiple Meanings of Words practice test (page 50). Give students 5–10 minutes to complete the test. Review the answers with the entire class.

Multiple Meanings of Words

Directions: Read each sentence. Choose the correct definition for each underlined word.

1. Most rocks are very light, but a boulder is quite heavy.

   (a) to set on fire

   (b) not dark in color

   (c) weighing very little

   (d) an electric lamp

2. The judge was very fair when she made her decision.

   (a) of light color

   (b) free of favoritism

   (c) lovely

   (d) where goods are sold

3. Finally, the baby went to sleep when the swing started to rock.

   (a) move back and forth

   (b) a stone

   (c) a heavy object

   (d) a type of loud music

4. Everyone cheered when the center fielder caught the fly to end the baseball game.

   (a) a winged insect

   (b) to move through the air

   (c) to pilot an aircraft

   (d) a ball that is batted in a high arc

5. It was a great distance from the foot of the mountain to the top.

   (a) measuring 12 inches

   (b) the base of an object

   (c) the lower end of a leg

   (d) an attachment for a sewing machine

6. Eight police officers tried to track the thief, but he got away.

   (a) follow

   (b) a rail on which trains run

   (c) a footprint

   (d) a sports event

7. Mr. Ruiz is only allowed to bring one small trunk on the airplane.

   (a) part of an elephant's body

   (b) men's swimming shorts

   (c) main part of a tree

   (d) a piece of luggage

8. I thought I had a perch on my fishing pole, but it was a turtle.

   (a) to sit on something

   (b) a small fish

   (c) a roost for a bird

   (d) a unit of cubic measurement

Test Prep with a Twist • Gr. 3 © 2003 Creative Teaching Press

Sweet Dream Pie

Written by Audrey Wood
Illustrated by Mark Teague
(Scholastic)

Synopsis

Ma and Pa Brindle get this sweet idea to concoct a rare dessert, Sweet Dream Pie. As the delicious ingredients get mixed together, things happen. Students will love reading about the neighborhood that gets turned upside down by the dangerously sugary dessert.

Activity

Copy a class set of the Sweet Synonym Pie reproducible onto card stock. Read *Sweet Dream Pie* to the class, and discuss the meaning of synonyms. Share with students how the author uses several words to describe "the big pie." Reread the story, and ask students to find all the synonyms for *big*. Invite volunteers to share their findings with the class. Record student responses on the board. Students should discover the words *extra large, enormous, great,* and *gigantic*. Give each student a Sweet Synonym Pie reproducible. Explain to the class that they will make their own "synonym pie." Have students begin by choosing six words from the board and writing one word in each section of Pie A. Then, have them write synonyms for the six words in each section of Pie B. For example, if a student chooses the word *happy*, he or she would write *happy* in one section of Pie A and words such as *content, glad,* and *joyful* in one section of Pie B. Once students have listed all the synonyms, have them cut around the outside of both pies and then set aside Pie B. Tell students to carefully cut on the dotted lines of each section of Pie A, making sure to stop cutting as soon as the dotted lines end. Give each student a brass fastener, and invite students to place Pie A on top of Pie B, with both sets of words faceup. Have students place their brass fastener through the solid dot on both pies. Tell them to color their synonym pie to make it look like a yummy pie. Invite volunteers to read their completed pie to the class.

Materials

• *Sweet Dream Pie*
• Sweet Synonym Pie reproducible (page 52)
• card stock
• scissors
• brass fasteners
• crayons or markers

Test Practice

Give each student a Synonyms practice test (page 53). Give students 5–10 minutes to complete the test. Review the answers with the entire class.

Sweet Synonym Pie

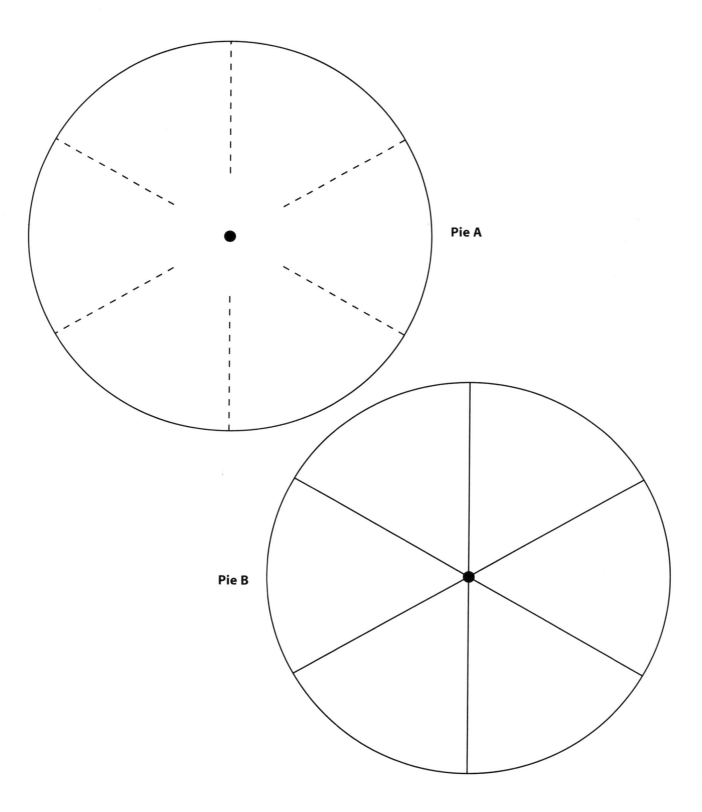

Pie A

Pie B

Test Prep with a Twist • Gr. 3 © 2003 Creative Teaching Press

Synonyms

Directions: Choose the synonym for the word in bold.

1. **hot**
   - (a) sizzling
   - (b) cool
   - (c) freezing
   - (d) chilly

2. **small**
   - (a) big
   - (b) huge
   - (c) giant
   - (d) tiny

3. **pretty**
   - (a) ugly
   - (b) scary
   - (c) beautiful
   - (d) hairy

4. **sweet**
   - (a) sour
   - (b) salty
   - (c) sugary
   - (d) bitter

5. **mad**
   - (a) happy
   - (b) angry
   - (c) excited
   - (d) old

6. **terrible**
   - (a) bad
   - (b) easy
   - (c) kind
   - (d) gentle

7. **silly**
   - (a) giggly
   - (b) easy
   - (c) kind
   - (d) gentle

8. **fast**
   - (a) slow
   - (b) jumpy
   - (c) quick
   - (d) sleepy

The Way I Feel

Written and illustrated by Janan Cain
(Scholastic)

Synopsis

This story uses vivid illustrations and a rhyming pattern to help children understand words that describe a person's feelings.

Activity

Read *The Way I Feel* to the class, and discuss how the text and illustrations help the reader understand the meaning of the words on each page. Copy and cut apart the Feeling Cards. Copy duplicate cards if needed so that each student has one card. Put the cards in a cup, and ask each student to randomly select one card. Have students use a dictionary to look up the meaning of their word, if needed. Give each student a large sheet of drawing paper. Tell students that they will draw the shoulders and head of a person and then add facial features that illustrate the meaning of the word that they selected. Have students write the word from their card in a sentence at the bottom of their paper. Challenge advanced students to write a rhyming sentence. Have each student share with the class his or her picture but not the sentence. Invite the class to guess what "feeling word" the picture describes. Once all students have shared their picture, collect the papers. Bind the pages together to create a class book.

Materials

- *The Way I Feel*
- Feeling Cards (page 55)
- scissors
- cup
- dictionaries
- drawing paper
- bookbinding materials

Test Practice

Give each student a Vocabulary Development practice test (page 56). Allow students 5–10 minutes to complete the test. Review the answers as a class.

Feeling Cards

angry	anxious	brave	confident
delighted	disgusted	eager	ecstatic
energetic	enthusiastic	frightened	frustrated
happy	honored	lucky	sad
scared	somber	sure	tired

Test Prep with a Twist • Gr. 3 © 2003 Creative Teaching Press

Name _____   Date _____

Vocabulary Development

Directions: Read each sentence. Choose the correct definition for each underlined word.

1. The boy told the teacher that his dog ate his homework. She thought that was an <u>absurd</u> excuse.

   (a) sad

   (b) ridiculous

   (c) creative

   (d) smart

2. The older woman smiled and told the young man that he was very <u>thoughtful</u> for carrying her groceries to her car.

   (a) considerate

   (b) careless

   (c) showing joy

   (d) determined

3. After training every day for the race, Bill was <u>confident</u> that he could win.

   (a) happy

   (b) eager

   (c) sure

   (d) full of energy

4. Since Ann was the star of the play, it was <u>crucial</u> for her to be at every practice on time. They could not start without her.

   (a) not possible

   (b) funny

   (c) not polite

   (d) very important

5. John was very <u>timid</u> and did not want to raise his hand to ask a question. He did not want to draw attention to himself.

   (a) small

   (b) big

   (c) shy

   (d) brave

6. Susan's mom told her not to go near the busy street because it is dangerous, so Susan <u>avoids</u> that street on her walk home from school.

   (a) smells

   (b) stays away from

   (c) sees

   (d) walks up to

Test Prep with a Twist • Gr. 3 © 2003 Creative Teaching Press

Name _____   Date _____

The Zoo

Directions: Read the story. Answer the following twelve questions.

A zoo is where you can see animals up close. You can also learn about each animal's habitat. Most of the animals at the zoo are wild. Some of them are endangered. This means that there are not many of those types of animals left in the world.

Sometimes, animals do not live long in the wild. They are hunted and killed. At the zoo, they are safe. Excellent zoos provide a large and safe home for each kind of animal. Zookeepers feed and take care of the animals. Zookeepers also clean the animals' living areas. The animals are well cared for at the zoo. How do zoos make homes for the animals? The zoo tries to make it look like the animals' habitats in the wild. Lions, giraffes, and zebras live in the grasslands. The grasslands are warm and dry. Elephants, monkeys, and toucans live in the jungle. The jungle is usually hot and wet. Bears and porcupines live in the forest. It is damp and cool there. Alligators live in a freshwater marsh. Grass and reeds grow out of the water in a marsh.

What if there were no zoos? Then people would not be able to see the animals up close and people would not be able to observe an animal's behavior.

1. What is the main idea of this passage?

   (a) Zoos are fun to visit.

   (b) People can learn about animals at the zoo.

   (c) Some zoos are very big.

   (d) Animals live in many places.

2. A grassland is _____.

   (a) damp and cool

   (b) hot and wet

   (c) warm and dry

   (d) icy and cold

3. In the first paragraph, which words help the reader know what <u>endangered</u> means?

   (a) in the wild

   (b) see animals up close

   (c) not many left

   (d) where they live

4. The most likely reason the author wrote this article was to _____.

   (a) explain the importance of zoos

   (b) tell about different animal habitats

   (c) persuade readers to visit the zoo

   (d) provide information about giraffes

Test Prep with a Twist · Gr. 3 © 2003 Creative Teaching Press

Name _____   Date _____

The Zoo

5. Which paragraph in the passage gives the reader details about habitats?

   (a) paragraph 1
   (b) paragraph 2
   (c) paragraph 3
   (d) not found in the passage

6. Which word is a **synonym** for <u>wild</u>?

   (a) gentle
   (b) mild
   (c) calm
   (d) untamed

7. Which word is an **antonym** for <u>warm</u>?

   (a) cool
   (b) hot
   (c) humid
   (d) cozy

8. What adjectives describe the jungle?

   (a) damp and cool
   (b) warm and dry
   (c) cold and wet
   (d) hot and wet

9. What is the effect of animals being hunted in the wild?

   (a) they do not live very long lives
   (b) they get to live in a zoo
   (c) people can learn about them
   (d) they get to eat

10. How many questions are found in the **last** paragraph?

    (a) 4
    (b) 3
    (c) 2
    (d) 1

11. Which word is a **synonym** for <u>damp</u>?

    (a) dry
    (b) cold
    (c) hot
    (d) wet

12. Which of the following is **not** a reason that animals are kept at zoos?

    (a) they are fed at the zoo
    (b) they are hunted at the zoo
    (c) their homes are clean at the zoo
    (d) they are safe at the zoo

Test Prep with a Twist • Gr. 3 © 2003 Creative Teaching Press

Name _____   Date _____

Alli and Abby

Directions: Read the story. Answer the following twelve questions.

Alli and Abby searched everywhere, but the tool for catching butterflies was gone. "Well, maybe if we don't look for it, it will just show up," Abby remarked. "It seems like all of our things keep disappearing," said Alli. Alli looked through the garage and found the fishing net. "This will work!" she exclaimed, and she set the net on top of the workbench.

After school, Alli fed her pet guinea pig and went out with her friend Abby to hunt for some colorful butterflies. They could hardly believe their eyes—the fishing net was gone! "Look!" shouted Abby. "Patch is digging in the sandbox." Now the mystery was solved, and they knew where to look for their lost items.

1. Read the chart below. It shows the order in which some of the events happened in the story.

The tool for catching butterflies was gone.
Alli found the fishing net in the garage.
Alli set the fishing net on the workbench and went to school.
Abby saw Patch digging.

    Which sentence belongs in the empty box?

    (a) Alli and Abby went to hunt for butterflies.

    (b) The mystery was solved.

    (c) The fishing net disappeared.

    (d) Alli searched through the garage.

2. What would be a good title for this story?

    (a) Best Friends Forever

    (b) Going Fishing

    (c) The Mystery of the Missing Objects

    (d) A Pet Guinea Pig

3. If during the next day, Alli's slipper is missing, where should the girls look for it?

    (a) in the garage

    (b) in the sandbox

    (c) at the beach

    (d) in the closet

Test Prep with a Twist • Gr. 3 © 2003 Creative Teaching Press

Alli and Abby

4. What event in the story helps the reader determine where the missing tools might be?

ⓐ Alli fed her pet guinea pig.

ⓑ Alli looked in the garage.

ⓒ They hunted for butterflies.

ⓓ Abby saw Patch digging in the sandbox.

5. What do you think the girls might do next?

ⓐ Catch ladybugs in a box.

ⓑ Look for worms.

ⓒ Search the sandbox for missing items.

ⓓ Play catch with Patch.

6. The contraction don't is a combination of what two words?

ⓐ does not

ⓑ did not

ⓒ do not

ⓓ will not

7. What is the **future** tense of the verb searched?

ⓐ searching

ⓑ search

ⓒ have searched

ⓓ will search

8. Which adjective best describes butterflies?

ⓐ sad

ⓑ mean

ⓒ colorful

ⓓ plain

9. Which word is a **synonym** for friend?

ⓐ enemy

ⓑ companion

ⓒ rival

ⓓ pet

10. Who are the **main** characters in this story?

ⓐ the butterflies

ⓑ the pet guinea pig

ⓒ Patch

ⓓ Alli and Abby

11. In this story, why is the word Patch capitalized?

ⓐ because Patch is a type of dog

ⓑ because the dog is digging

ⓒ because it is the specific name of the dog

ⓓ because Abby is shouting

12. What is the setting in this story?

ⓐ school and Alli's room

ⓑ the beach and in the house

ⓒ the garage and outside

ⓓ Patch's doghouse

Test Prep with a Twist • Gr. 3 © 2003 Creative Teaching Press

Name _____ Date _____

Apple Crisp

Directions: Read the recipe. Answer the following twelve questions.

Apple Crisp

Ingredients

2 medium apples, pared and sliced
2 tablespoons sugar
2 tablespoons water
3 tablespoons flour
2 tablespoons butter, softened
¼ teaspoon ground cinnamon

Directions

Heat oven to 350 degrees. Put apple slices in a baking dish. Sprinkle water over apple slices. Mix the butter, sugar, flour, and cinnamon with a fork until crumbly; sprinkle over apples. Bake uncovered for 25 to 30 minutes until the topping is light brown and the apples are tender. Makes 2 servings.

1. After reading the recipe, what can you conclude the word <u>pared</u> means?
   - (a) to arrange in sets of two
   - (b) to remove an outer skin
   - (c) to provide a partner
   - (d) to join together

2. The last step is to _____.
   - (a) sprinkle water over the apples
   - (b) bake for 25–30 minutes
   - (c) heat the oven to 350 degrees
   - (d) put apple slices in a baking dish

3. What would be the **best** way to determine if the apples were tender?
   - (a) prick them with a fork
   - (b) bite into a very hot apple slice
   - (c) wait until you can smell the apple crisp cooking
   - (d) there is no good way to tell

4. What do you think might happen if you baked the apple crisp for 50 minutes?
   - (a) it would still be cold in the middle
   - (b) the butter would not melt
   - (c) it would make additional servings
   - (d) it might burn

Final Review Tests

Apple Crisp

5. Which two adjectives describe this dessert?
   - (a) yummy recipe
   - (b) light brown
   - (c) warm and tasty
   - (d) pared and sliced

6. The contraction here's is a combination of what two words?
   - (a) how is
   - (b) here is
   - (c) where is
   - (d) she is

7. What is the **past** tense of the verb sprinkle?
   - (a) will sprinkle
   - (b) sprinkler
   - (c) sprinkled
   - (d) sprinklest

8. In this recipe, the word ground means _____.
   - (a) soil; earth
   - (b) the land surrounding a house
   - (c) the sediment at the bottom of a liquid (for example, coffee grinds)
   - (d) crushed; powdered

9. Which word is a **synonym** for tender?
   - (a) soft
   - (b) rough
   - (c) sweet
   - (d) dry

10. In the fifth sentence of the recipe directions, what is the adjective that describes the topping?
    - (a) light brown
    - (b) uncovered
    - (c) tender
    - (d) crumbly

11. Which word is an **antonym** for crumbly?
    - (a) powdery
    - (b) wet
    - (c) solid
    - (d) tasty

12. In this recipe, the word flour refers to _____.
    - (a) part of a plant
    - (b) a soft powder used in baking
    - (c) to develop or mature
    - (d) a rose

Test Prep with a Twist · Gr. 3 © 2003 Creative Teaching Press

Answer Key

Page 10
1. c
2. b
3. a
4. d
5. d
6. a
7. c
8. b

Page 17
1. c
2. a
3. b
4. d
5. d
6. b

Page 24
1. c
2. a
3. c
4. d
5. b
6. a
7. b
8. d

Page 31
1. a
2. b
3. b
4. d
5. c
6. b

Page 12
1. d
2. b
3. d
4. a
5. c
6. d

Page 19
1. a
2. c
3. b
4. d
5. a
6. b

Page 27
1. d
2. c
3. c
4. b
5. b
6. a
7. d
8. b

Page 33
1. c
2. b
3. a
4. c
5. b
6. c
7. d
8. d

Page 14
1. c
2. b
3. a
4. d
5. d
6. d

Page 21
1. d
2. b
3. c
4. a
5. b
6. c
7. c
8. b

Page 29
1. b
2. c
3. a
4. b
5. d
6. a
7. a
8. d

Page 36
1. b
2. c
3. d
4. a
5. b
6. c
7. a
8. c

Answer Key

Page 38
1. b
2. d
3. d
4. b
5. a
6. b
7. a
8. d

Page 41
1. b
2. c
3. b
4. a
5. b
6. d
7. a
8. d

Page 43
1. c
2. b
3. a
4. d
5. c
6. a
7. b
8. d

Page 45
1. b
2. a
3. b
4. d
5. c
6. d
7. b
8. a

Page 48
1. d
2. b
3. c
4. a
5. b
6. b
7. a
8. d

Page 50
1. c
2. b
3. a
4. d
5. b
6. a
7. d
8. b

Page 53
1. a
2. d
3. c
4. c
5. b
6. a
7. a
8. c

Page 56
1. b
2. a
3. c
4. d
5. c
6. b

Pages 57–58
1. b
2. c
3. c
4. a
5. b
6. d
7. a
8. d
9. a
10. d
11. d
12. b

Pages 59–60
1. c
2. c
3. b
4. d
5. c
6. c
7. d
8. c
9. b
10. d
11. c
12. c

Pages 61–62
1. b
2. b
3. a
4. d
5. c
6. b
7. c
8. d
9. a
10. a
11. c
12. b